Diary of a Zombie Steve

······································

Book 1

MC Steve

© Copyright 2016 by Leopard Books LLC - All rights reserved.

No part of this publication may be reproduced or transmitted in any form whatsoever, electronic, or mechanical, including photocopying, recording, or by any informational storage or retrieval system without express written, dated and signed permission from the author.

This book is a work of fan fiction; it is not an official Minecraft book. It is not endorsed, authorized, licensed, sponsored, or supported by Mojang AB, Microsoft Corp. or any other entity owning or controlling rights to the Minecraft name, trademarks or copyrights.

Minecraft ®/TM & © 2009-2016 Mojang / Notch / Microsoft

Table of Contents

Saturday
ZFC Training Field.. 5

Sunday
Home and Village.. 7

Monday
Work.. 12

Tuesday
Wolfe Forest and Work.. 14

Wednesday
Wolfe Forest... 21

Thursday
Vale of Spiders... 29

Friday
Bunny Hill.. 32

Saturday
Abandoned Jungle Fortress and the Snow Plains.................. 35

Sunday
Snow Plains... 44

Monday
Bone Yard 47

Tuesday
Inside Rainbow Mesa 55

Wednesday
Deep Inside Rainbow Mesa 57

Thursday
Still Deep Inside Rainbow Mesa 60

Friday
Inside Rainbow Mesa 63

Saturday
Outside Rainbow Mesa 64

Sunday
Valhalla Prison 66

Monday
Valhalla Prison 67

Tuesday
Home 68

Saturday - ZFC Training Field

Saturday
ZFC Training Field

Zombie Steve here. After eating a breakfast of mud grits and swamp water coffee, I was off to training in the official ZFC training field. ZFC stands for Zombie Fright Coalition, and I am an active member. Once a month we spend an entire evening practicing our scaring skills. Tonight we did quite a bit. We started off with moaning practice (no zombie is worth his salt if he can't terrify a miner with just one moan) followed by advanced door rattling (nothing creeps out villagers like rattling and banging on their door). Next we worked on our evasion techniques for when we get cornered or are being pursued. This is especially important for when a village hires an iron golem or a professional zombie hunter. Finally we had to work on our intellects. Each one of us (there are twenty of us in this coalition) had to give a five minute presentation on the history of zombies. Mine was about Herobrine and how many of us zombies claim him as one of our own.

Well, after all that, I, for one, had worked up quite an appetite, but I had to go straight to work. I was hired last week by Zombies of the World Insurance Agency to expand their current offices, which are located in Poppy's Peak Mountain. I make a good living doing excavation and architecture to build homes and offices out of stone mountains. I actually started in this line of work after I scared a miner so bad he caused a cave-in. He was on the outside of the cave-in, but I was on the inside. I took one of his extra pickaxes and carved my way out and discovered that I really liked working with stone. But that's a story for another day.

 Diary of a Zombie Steve — Book 1

When I finally got off work (and thankfully I didn't wake up any of those annoying silverfish in the process), I headed home. I was so tired I just fixed a seaweed sandwich with some swamp water tea. I'm about to go to bed now. It's been daylight for an hour, so it's awfully late for me. Goodnight, diary.

Sunday
Home and Village

Zombie Steve here. Today was my day off, so I could do whatever I wanted (within reason, of course). First I wanted to sleep in. I slept until about an hour after sunset, which was awfully late for me, but it didn't matter because I didn't need to be anywhere. I got out of bed, wrinkled my clothes, and mussed up my hair.

Next I ate a healthy zombie breakfast of spoiled ivy in swamp slime with a mud drink for energy. I live in an awesome cave studio apartment that I hewed out myself. It has a nice, soft gravel bed with green wool carpet. It has a furnace to keep it warm in the wintertime and to cook my meals on.

I also have some cool stuff I collected after scaring miners out of the nearby caves.

My next destination was to meet some buddies of mine—Zombie Bart and Archie the Skeleton—to have a few hours of scaring villagers. We've been scaring in this village since we were little baby zombies.

Here's the thing I don't understand: The villagers know that we come to their village on a regular basis, but they still either one, hang around outside at night, or two, act terrified like they have never seen a zombie in their life.

Diary of a Zombie Steve — Book 1

Of course, two I don't mind—that's fun. I do mind one. I once scared a villager so bad he fell in the well. I couldn't leave him in there to drown, you know. I risked my reputation as a zombie to pull the guy out.

Sunday - Home and Village

When I did get him out, he fainted. Now, if you think a fainted villager is a lot of dead weight to drag around, try one that is sopping wet with well water! Anyways, humans smell awfully funny when they get wet. Well, to get on with my story, I dragged him out of the well and into a nearby field so someone would see him and help him. Fortunately the villagers thought I was eating him and rushed right out. Some zombies, I hate to say, would have taken advantage of the situation. I am a new-age zombie though: we scare, but we care.

Bart, Archie, and I headed to the village and did our usual scaring. We started with the local library. That librarian has read so many scary stories all we need to do is peek in the window and he runs for cover. I noticed on the side of the library a sign I hadn't seen before. It said this: "REWARD! Lost child. See picture below. Please return to the Valhalla Compound."

I pointed it out to Archie, who was standing nearby. "Hey, Archie! Have you seen this kid?"

"Yep," replied Archie, "every time I see a kid. All those human villager kids look just alike."

"I know, right? I hope they can tell them apart better than we can, or there's going to be a lot of kids being taken to the Valhalla Compound," I replied.

"Valhalla Compound?" asked Bart with a little bit of concern in his voice. "That's no place for the likes of us. What are you saying about it?"

"Reward," I answered as I pointed to the sign.

"Well, the reward they would have for the likes of us isn't one I'd want. The guy in charge of that compound is General Peter Fightem, AZ Division."

"Wow," I replied. The AZ Division is the Anti-Zombie Division. They don't like us at all.

Sunday - Home and Village

Archie chimed in again, "Well, I think it's probably a trap or something. I heard that since you zombies have gone modern with your 'we scare, but we care' lifestyle they don't have much grounds to hunt you guys anymore. They're probably trying to drum up some business."

We all nodded our heads and noticed the librarian peeking out. We peeked in at him. He screamed and hid again.

After we finished scaring I headed back to my cave studio apartment and worked on adding some additional storage shelves for my collection of things left behind by scared miners. I have four different types of swords, a stale loaf of broad, two ingots of iron, an entire block of coal, four paintings, some wool rugs, and several pieces of armor.

Well, I'm worn out now and heading to bed. Goodnight, diary.

 Diary of a Zombie Steve — Book 1

Monday
Work

Zombie Steve here. Well, today was a busy day. I had to put in quite a bit of overtime at work today. You see, I was hired to design and build a doctor's office for the skeleton archers. You see, sometimes when they are out at night scaring people and guarding treasures, they might lose a bone or two. One of the archers, Dr. Tibia, has decided to start a treatment center for them and hired me.

Here is the problem: Dr. Tibia wants everything yesterday, by which I mean he wants things unreasonably quickly. I didn't even have any time to scare tonight! I just worked, worked, worked. He wanted it built in the side of Noble Mountain. That was okay until I ran right into a vein of iron. I love finding iron, but not when I am in a hurry. It takes longer for me to mine and wears out my tools too quickly. I finally got past the iron ore and ran straight into a cavern that drops off into a very deep underground lake of lava. Yes, you read that correctly: a lava lake!

Well, to be safe I had to first create a floor covering the lava lake, then double its thickness just to make sure no one accidentally creates an opening to the lava pit below. Once I got that finished I had the waiting room done. It had a much higher ceiling than I had originally designed for, but it looked pretty cool. It will look especially cool after I add some jack-o'-lantern lighting.

Monday - Work

Well, I thought I would get off in time to do a little bit of scaring, but that didn't work out either. Just as I got the waiting room finished and was going to build the office areas, there was a minor cave-in. Gravel cave-ins are bad, but sand cave-ins are even worse. You get sand in places you didn't know it could get! Two months after one sand cave-in I was still trying to get the sand out of my ears. So I had a minor sand cave-in that I had to clean up before I could keep working, which ate up all my scaring time.

I guess what started out as stating facts turned into complaining! Oh well, maybe I can schedule some scaring time tomorrow if I spend a little extra time in my cave tonight working on the revised plans for Dr. Tibia's office. I just hope he hasn't changed his mind about anything!

Talk to you later, diary.

 Diary of a Zombie Steve — Book 1

Tuesday
Wolfe Forest and Work

Zombie Steve here. I managed to free up some time so I could go scaring with my friends this evening. That was the start of one of the most unusual days in my entire life.

It seems that a little boy named Beep sneaked off from a school field trip that was visiting our local library—you know, the one with the cowardly librarian. Beep decided to follow a lone rabbit he saw by the side of the library, and before he knew it Beep found himself in the middle of what we call Wolfe Forest. We call it that because it is the domain of a pack of very wild, unfriendly wolves.

Well, it so happens to be that where my buddies and I meet up to terrorize our local villagers is right next to Wolfe Forest. So there we were, minding our own business, making some rough plans for what we were going to do to the villagers that night. Archie and Bart were discussing the librarian when we suddenly heard a terrifying sound coming from Wolfe Forest. It was the sound of a child's laughter.

Mind you, it was dark outside, and no human in his or her right mind was going to be in Wolfe Forest or anywhere outside. What was even scarier was that the sound was that of a child. Never had we ever heard a child out in the dark before. It's simply not done! Never, ever, ever does anyone leave a child out in the darkness of night.

Tuesday - Wolfe Forest and Work

Archie and Bart screamed like little girls. I screamed like a little boy. The point is it scared us so badly we lost all of our dignity and bearing as fearsome creatures of the night. The source of this sound could be one thing and one thing only: a GHOST!

None of us had ever seen a ghost, although we were pretty sure we had heard a few. Frankly we never hung around long enough to see a ghost if one was there. We can move pretty fast when we need to. Forget the image of the slow, lumbering, uncoordinated zombie pursuing someone. Picture instead a sleek, fast, highly coordinated, high-speed zombie. That's what you see when a zombie thinks it hears a ghost.

Archie and Bart ran, but I will be completely honest: for a split second, I was so scared I couldn't move. That's why I didn't join Archie and Bart. When I did come to my senses, still hearing the laughter, I decided that a ghost kid couldn't be that scary. I summoned all the courage I had left in me and turned toward the forest. If there was a ghost, I wanted to see it!

Slowly I crept between the trees until I was at the edge of a clearing. There I saw the leader of the wolf pack, Howler. Howler is a big, ragged, rough-looking wolf whose red eyes strike fear into the heart of anything he encounters. Well, anything but this kid ghost.

I almost laughed when I saw what was going on. This ghost kid—or actual kid, as it turned out—was poking Howler in the stomach with a soft branch. Howler was jumping around trying to get away from the kid, but it didn't do any good. That little kid could outmaneuver him.

Well, at the time I still thought he was a ghost. Howler is my friend. He helped me out once when I accidentally angered a pack of about twenty silverfish, but that's a story for another time. The point is that I knew Howler was being tormented and humiliated. There were some other wolves around the clearing, and I could tell by the snorting sounds I heard that they were trying not to laugh. This just wasn't right, so I once again summoned all my courage up and forged into the clearing.

Tuesday - Wolfe Forest and Work

I moaned, groaned, growled, and stuck my arms out in front of me menacingly. Surely my most fearsome zombie visage would be enough to temporarily stun this unruly child ghost.

The child ghost turned around and looked at me. I was expecting fear to be in his eyes as he staggered backward in terror. Instead he smiled from ear to ear and let out another wild laugh.

Howler took this opportunity to grab the stick that the kid had been poking him with and toss it into the forest. I continued to growl and draw closer to the child. He continued to smile at me, and instead of running away from me in fear, he ran toward me and hugged my leg.

Hugged my leg! I was never so terrified. Keep in mind I still thought the little guy was a ghost. Was this how ghosts killed zombies? Was he trying to take possession of me? What was his evil master plan?

Now Howler and his pack, who had all entered the clearing, were laughing. I tried to shake the little monster off my leg, but when I did he seemed to think it was great fun and started laughing too.

I am one of the most fearsome zombies in the whole world, and there I was in the middle of a clearing in the woods with some *thing* hanging on my leg for all he was worth while I tried to shake it off. I was humiliated, scared, and puzzled.

Between roars of laughter, Howler finally spoke up: "Steve, the little human kid seems to like you!"

I stopped shaking my leg. "It's a real kid? For real?" I asked.

Howler responded, "Indeed it is, and as it seems he has bonded with you, YOU get to keep him!"

 Diary of a Zombie Steve — Book 1

Another wolf chimed in, "Whatcha gonna name him, Zombie Steve?"

I growled and tried to shake the kid off again. He gripped my leg even tighter and laughed louder. When I growled it seemed to frighten the wolves a bit (as it should), and they all backed up. I finally reached down and peeled the short arms and legs off my leg (which would be losing circulation by now if I weren't a zombie) and lifted him up in the air. I made sure he couldn't reach me and took a good look at him.

He looked like every other little kid I had ever seen. "What's your name, kid?"

"Beep!" was his reply, and he kicked his legs and tried to get loose. He wasn't getting free from my grasp anytime soon. Howler and I had both been humiliated enough.

"Why aren't you afraid of me, Beep?"

"What's to be afraid of? I think you're cool!" he said with emphasis on the word "cool."

"What about the wolf? Why'd you keep poking him, ya little brat?"

"'Cause I wanted him to roll over so I could pet his soft tummy."

I could hear suppressed laughs and giggles from everyone in the wolf pack but Howler. Howler was shaking his head.

"You need to go home, kid. It isn't safe out here. Where do you live?"

"Valor Holler."

Tuesday - Wolfe Forest and Work

"I never heard of it, kid. How far away is it?"

"Sixteen candy bars."

"Sixteen candy bars? What the jelly bean is sixteen candy bars supposed to mean?"

Howler piped in. "I think he was able to eat sixteen large candy bars between here and his home. Look at what fell out of his pocket."

There, on the ground beneath Beep, was a pile of extremely large candy bar wrappers.

"Which way, kid?" I asked.

"I dunno" was his reply.

I looked at Howler. "We can't leave him out here. He won't last too long."

Howler shook his massive head. "Don't look at me like that, Steve. I'm not a babysitter! He's closer to your species. You take him!"

I looked down at the weird little kid hanging on my leg. "Okay, I'll take him with me, then leave him out tomorrow for his people to find him." I reached down and gingerly pet him on his head. His hair was brown and soft. "Okay, kiddo. You're coming to work with me."

I then proceeded to walk to work with a human child hanging on my leg, giggling incessantly. We arrived at Dr. Tibia's office—well, the future location of Dr. Tibia's office. I opened the door I had installed last week and locked it so Beep

 Diary of a Zombie Steve — Book 1

couldn't get out and cause trouble. I started finishing up the waiting room when I accidentally hit a silverfish block. About four silverfish poured out, and Beep started chasing them all over the place. I finally found something that unnerves silverfish: Beep!

"Yo, Zombie Steve, call off ya guard dog already!" yelled Slick, one of the younger silverfish.

"That's just a little boy, you cowards," I replied with a chuckle.

"Well, make him quit chasing me and grabbing my tail! I can't go back in the rock with a little monster hanging on my tail!"

I called out to Beep, "Let him go, Beep. It isn't nice to pull silverfish tails."

Beep replied, still holding on to Slick's tail, "Do I gotta?"

"Yeah, kid, ya gotta." He let go, allowing Slick to disappear back in the rock.

It got real quiet all of a sudden. I got worried. I looked around, and there was Beep, sound asleep on a rock. I felt kind of bad for him, so I took my shirt off and covered him up with it. When I finished work he was still sound asleep, so I carried him home.

My plan was to leave him out in the forest at the break of dawn so some human could find him and take him home.

Wednesday - Wolfe Forest

Wednesday
Wolfe Forest

As soon as daylight began to break, I took Beep outside (he was still sound asleep) and laid him on the ground near a well traveled path. I was really risking a sunburn, but I couldn't leave him without making sure he'd be safe enough. I hid behind some really thick trees and watched. Some wolves were nearby, doing what wolves do. Well, Beep woke up, stretched, and headed right for the wolves.

Before I could say a word, he was petting them again! Risking sunburn, I ran back to my cave apartment and grabbed some steak. I ran back out, this time getting a sunburn, and used the steak to tame one of the wolf pups.

Actually though, I gave it to Beep and told him to feed it to the wolf pup. They became instant friends, and Beep said he was naming his wolf pup Killer.

Howler called out a hearty "thank you," and they agreed to help keep an eye out for Beep.

I was still under a tree, developing a slight sunburn. I gave Killer orders to protect Beep, and he agreed. I headed back to my cave to get some much needed sleep. About ten minutes later there was a howl at my door. It was Howler.

Diary of a Zombie Steve — Book 1

"Your little monster is in the lake with Killer (his real name is Fluffy Butt, by the way, Steve) playing wrestling match with the squid."

Wednesday - Wolfe Forest

I sighed, got out of bed, and made a sign for anyone looking for Beep to come to my place. I then covered up with a blanket to protect myself from the sun and with Howler's help got Beep and Killer Fluffy Butt back to my cave.

Back in the cave, I locked the door so Beep couldn't get out and tried to find something to do. It turns out I had some old buckets of paint, so I quickly carved out a little room for Beep and told him to decorate it. Killer had orders to wake me if Beep got into trouble, and I fell into bed and fell asleep.

After a few hours a little hand shook me. I rolled over and screamed. Beep was so covered in paint he didn't look human or monster! It seemed he'd gotten more paint on himself than he did on the walls, but he was very proud and wanted me see his work. I was quite impressed and told him so.

Now he was hungry, so I fixed a steak for Beep and Killer. I was about to try to find something for them to do when I realized they were having a blast playing with each other. I doze off for a few hours, and then I heard a knock at the door.

Hoping against hope it was his parents or his teacher, I answered the door. I knew that old man standing there. I could recognize the stench of swamp water on him anywhere. It was the witch Walnut, who was claiming to be Beep's uncle. I asked Beep if this was his uncle.

"Do you have any candy bars?" Beep asked him. The little rascal! I pushed Walnut back out the door and locked it again.

"He might have been my uncle!" said Beep with great indignation. "And he might have had some candy."

Diary of a Zombie Steve — Book 1

"Beep, there are bad people out in the world. You can't trust everybody. It's like, you can't just go up to some wolf and pet its tummy or to a zombie like me and grab its leg. Someone might hurt you, little guy."

Wednesday - Wolfe Forest

"You didn't!" pointed out Beep. He was standing in front of me with his hands on his hips. Killer Fluffy Butt was sitting beside him, nodding his head in agreement.

"You were lucky to find some nice guys like me and Howler and Killer. But not everybody is nice. You need to be careful. And tell me again, kiddo, what's the name of your village?"

"It's called Vale Holler."

"Never heard of it. Let's take a look at my map."

I pulled out my map and started looking at all the nearby villages, moving farther and farther out until I finally found something that looked like what Beep had been pronouncing.

I inwardly groaned. Apparently my little friend was from Valhalla, which meant he was probably the missing boy from the poster. But he couldn't be!

"Beep, are you from Valhalla?"

"Yeah, that's what I said, wasn't it?"

I had him sit down at the table with me. "How did you get here, Beep?" I don't know why I hadn't asked that earlier.

"These men said they were my new teachers and were taking me on a field trip. It was a long field trip, and I started crying for my mom and my dad 'cause I missed them. They gave me some candy bars to get me to quit crying. Well, after we had been gone about two days I wanted to know why we hadn't gone anywhere interesting on this field trip! All we'd done was walk and walk and walk. They got really mad at me for some stuff I had done, like setting a tree branch on fire with lava and chasing some bunny rabbits. Well, when we got to the woods they told me to stay there and play with the wolves. They left me there, and I was playing with the wolves when you found me!"

It made sense to me that little Beep could drive some kidnappers crazy, and that's just what I suspected those men were: rotten, good-for-nothing kidnappers. So here I was, a zombie with a kid that might just belong to a notorious zombie hunter. He needed to go home to Valhalla, but how could I take him?

I noticed it was getting close to time for me to go to work. I decided to take Beep with me back to Dr. Tibia's office (still a work in progress). I noticed a stone I figured was a silverfish block, so I hit it on purpose to provide little Beep and Killer with some entertainment. This time it wasn't Slick but his grandpa Sly Willie. Sly Willie seemed to have fun playing around with Beep.

While I worked, little Beep either played or slept. I had picked up some potatoes for them out of a field on the way to work and rigged up a simple stove so I could make us all some baked potatoes while I worked. The whole time I worked I worried:

How could Beep safely get home, seeing as he was kidnapped in the first place?

I heard a knock at Dr. Tibia's new office door and peeked out. It was Bart and Archie. Bart spoke up first. "Tell us you don't have that monstrosity in there!"

"The kid? Yeah, and if you don't keep it down he'll wake up and make us all miserable. Why?" was my reply. As harsh as it may sound, I was actually smiling when I said it.

Wednesday - Wolfe Forest

"Are you crazy? The head of the zombie hunters is looking for that kid! If someone human sees you with it, it'll be the end of you!" whispered Archie, not too quietly. "I think he's the kid on the flyer we saw. He's trouble."

"Well, someone needs to take him home," I replied.

"Not you, Zombie Steve. He's not your responsibility. Leave him in the village over there and be done with it," hissed Bart.

I could hear Beep stirring inside. "Guys, I need to go back in. If we leave him in the village, there's a chance that he might fall into the wrong hands. The sign says to take him to Valhalla, and that's what I'm going to do."

Archie and Bart both shook their heads. "We figured you'd say that, so we stocked up on some veggies and melons from the village tonight. You know, they don't eat as healthy as we do, and their bodies just aren't used to our fine dining. Here," said Bart, and he handed me a large bag heavy with food.

"Thanks, guys. You want to come along?" I could hear Beep coming close to the door.

"No, Steve-o, this is your quest."

"Are you sure?" I was actually delaying a moment. I was pretty sure that in about half a second Beep would start jumping up and down to see out the window on my door. And he did!

Archie and Bart screamed and ran, and I almost fell over laughing. I opened the door, greeted Beep, and we ate the baked potatoes I had been cooking. Beep wanted to know what was in my bag.

 Diary of a Zombie Steve — Book 1

"Provisions for our adventure that starts tomorrow evening."

"All right!" he squealed with delight, and little Killer laughed and joined in with a howl.

I wish I could be as happy as they are, but I'm still awfully worried. Oh well! Until tomorrow night, diary.

Thursday
Vale of Spiders

Zombie Steve here. Well, Beep, Killer, and I started on our journey toward Valhalla. If I wrote down every disaster Beep almost caused while we were journeying tonight I would run out of pages really fast. I'll only talk about one of them.

There is a wide desert plain with some scattered cactuses and lots of spiders. It's known as the Vale of Spiders. Humans are creeped out by spiders and try to avoid it, but seeing as I am a zombie and I scare things, not let things scare me, I decided to take advantage of it as a shortcut to Valhalla.

Well, we didn't get very far tonight because Beep noticed the spiders. If you're thinking he was afraid of them you're way off. He noticed they were furry and decided they must be something to pet! Before Killer or I could do anything, Beep was petting one of the spiders.

Now, here's something that most people don't know about spiders in the desert: they are terrified of humans, almost to the point of it being a phobia. When Beep ran over there and started to pet that spider, whose name we learned was Floyd, that spider froze in absolute terror.

As Killer and I ran toward Beep and started calling to him to leave that poor spider alone, Beep climbed up on the spider's back like it was a horse.

 Diary of a Zombie Steve — Book 1

Yes, you heard me: like it was a horse. Floyd screamed a most bone-chilling scream, then yelled, "Get it off! Get it off! Please, somebody get it off!"

I grabbed Beep's shirt, and Killer grabbed his leg, and Beep came off the spider. Floyd fell on the ground, crying. "Why would you bring that monster out here?"

"I'm sorry, sir. He got away from me."

"And he got on me!" he whined, still crying.

"Beep, apologize to...uh, sir, what's your name?"

"Floyd!" the spider wailed.

"Apologize to Floyd for scaring him."

Beep looked up at me. "I scared him?"

"Why do you think he screamed, Beep? Now apologize."

Beep giggled. "Mr. Floyd, I am very sorry I scared you. Please accept my sincere apologies."

It sounded like Beep was in the habit of apologizing!

"Fine, just take that little monster and get him out of here!" cried Floyd. "Here, take this," he continued, tossing me a length of spider silk. "It makes a good rope. If you are going to bring a dangerous creature like that into the Vale of the Spiders, we have leash laws."

Thursday - Vale of Spiders

"Thanks," I said as I tied it around Beep's waist and held it in my hand. Killer Fluffy Butt got awfully tickled seeing Beep tied up like a dog.

We then proceeded across the Vale, with Beep pulling and tugging on the "leash" until he just about wore me out. I finally stopped a few hours before dawn, earlier than I intended to but too tired to wrestle with Beep anymore.

We ate a good meal of carrots and melon, and then I quickly carved out a makeshift shelter for us in the side of a hill. I added a door, locked it, and made us some nice, soft dirt beds.

That's it for tonight, diary.

Diary of a Zombie Steve — Book 1

Friday
Bunny Hill

Zombie Steve here. We crossed the Vale of Spiders early this evening and reached a river. I had noticed something smelling really, really bad. I know that people think zombies smell, and maybe we do, but whatever I smelled was a thousand times worse than the smelliest zombie I'd ever encountered. As our little group sat down to eat I sniffed the air.

"What is it, Boss?" asked Killer. He had taken to calling me Boss.

"Something stinks really bad," I replied. I sniffed in his direction.

"Well, don't look at me, Boss. I can tell you what smells so bad!" We both looked over at Beep. He grinned at us. Beep was so nasty-looking you could swear he was a zombie, which was fine with me, but there was an unbearable stench that went with his appearance.

I looked over at Killer. "Are you thinking what I'm thinking, Killer?"

Killer wagged his tail. "Yeah, Boss." We both looked over at Beep as he took his last swallow of food.

"What? Oh no, no, no, no, no, no! Not a...not a..."

Friday - Bunny Hill

Killer and I finished his sentence at the same time: "Bath!"

We rushed him and dragged him to a shallow pond that had formed near the river. We threw him in, and every time he got out we tossed him back in. Killer finally jumped in with him, and Beep decided the water wasn't so bad. We got him out, dried him off, and I quickly made him a pair of leaf pants to wear for modesty while we dried his clothes over a quick oven I set up. I also made a little hair comb for him out of a twig, and made his hair lie down better.

Even as a zombie I have to admit that between the stench he put off and his hair, he was a bit scary-looking. As soon as his clothes dried we headed on to our next destination: Bunny Hill.

Honestly I should have known better than to try to take another shortcut via a place called Bunny Hill. There is a huge pack of rabbits that live there. They are very nervous, jumpy, hyperactive rabbits. And I have a hyper, curious, ornery little human boy and a wolf pup. This was a recipe for disaster, and I should have known it.

As soon as Beep and Killer caught sight of a bunny at the base of the hill, the chaos began.

Let's just say it took an hour to catch Beep and Killer both, another hour to apologize to the rabbits, and thirty minutes to get all that fur from between Killer's teeth. Now, he didn't hurt any of them, but he did nip at them enough to get several mouthfuls of rabbit fluff. He looked like he had grown a multicolored mustache with all that fur hanging out when he opened his mouth. It just looked...disturbing.

Well, by the time we got everything resolved and were summarily chased off Bunny Hill by its rightful residents, it was almost morning. I again made us a temporary shelter in the side of a nearby hill (not Bunny Hill!), and we called it a night. This kid is wearing me out!

Saturday

Abandoned Jungle Fortress and the Snow Plains

Beep got out of the shelter I made last night. I woke up and glanced over, and he wasn't there, and neither was Killer, his wolf pup. I unlocked the door and stuck my head out. No sign of Beep anywhere. I started to call out for him when I heard a rattling sound. It was a skeleton archer, but not one like my friend. This was a distinct kind of rattle. It was one of the Bone Men.

The Bone Men are a group of notorious mercenaries, villains for hire ready to work for anyone who has enough money. I figured that there was a good chance that Beep's kidnappers had hired them to retrieve Beep. I felt a bit sorry for the Bone Men: they had no idea what they'd gotten themselves into when it came to Beep.

Quietly I followed the rattling sound and soon came upon a long-forgotten jungle fortress built into the side of a tall cliff. I could see, through the open windows, the Bone Men inside. I quietly made my way around, trying to figure out how I was going to get Beep back. I was pretty quiet too until I accidentally stepped on that ocelot's tail.

"Yowza!" it cried out.

 Diary of a Zombie Steve — Book 1

"Ssshhhh!" I whispered back to it.

"Stop shushing me, you big klutz! You stepped on my TAIL!"

"I'm sorry, but please don't give my position away!" I whispered back to it, pointing in the general direction of the Bone Men. I continued, "My name is Zombie Steve, and I am trying to rescue that little kid in there!"

"Well, my name is Hobo, and my tail still hurts" was the lean ocelot's reply.

"I am very sorry. I didn't see it."

"Why are you trying to get that little monstrosity?" asked Hobo.

"I found him a few days ago, and I'm trying to get him back to his family."

"I don't think creatures like him have a family!" hissed Hobo.

"What did he do?" I asked, sure that Beep had already met my new acquaintance.

"Well, I was napping in that tree over there when the little rascal tied a tree branch to my tail. That annoying giggle sound he makes woke me up, and when I stretched the tree branch startled me. I chased it for an hour." Hobo moved so close to my face I could feel his whiskers on my cheeks. "I chased it FOR AN HOUR. Things like that little creature shouldn't be free to run loose in the forest. Tell me how I can help you get him back home to his parents and I'll help."

I was trying really hard not to laugh at the thought of this big, sleek, dangerous-looking ocelot chasing a tree branch tied to his tail for an hour. I didn't dare

Saturday - Abandoned Jungle Fortress and the Snow Plains

laugh though. I put on my most serious face. "Well, I'm trying to figure out how to get him out of there," I replied, pointing toward the jungle fortress.

The ocelot turned and looked. "I know a secret way in. Follow me, and whatever you do, DON'T STEP ON MY TAIL. Or tie anything to it."

Quietly we made our way toward the back of the cliff that the fortress was built into. Hobo effortlessly leaped onto a tree branch and motioned for me to follow. After some difficulty I climbed onto the tree branch. When I finally got up there Hobo was tapping one toenail on the tree trunk impatiently. "Sometime this year, Zombie Boy. Now, we are going to make a jump for that opening."

My gaze followed Hobo's outstretched paw. It was a big jump, to say the least. If I missed I'd land on some uncomfortable rocky outcroppings. But I'm a big zombie, and I do big things. I stepped back and made the jump. I landed in a dark tunnel. I could hear gravel crunching beneath my feet. In a moment Hobo landed beside me.

"Not bad for a zombie," he said. "Now, follow me."

As we made our way through the darkness I could hear the rattling sounds of the Bone Men getting closer and closer. I could also hear Beep giggle, but not as much as usual. This concerned me.

I could see light ahead. We had reached the end of the tunnel. It opened up into a large room surrounded by the open windows I saw earlier. In the middle was little Beep, and he had Killer Fluffy Butt by his side. Killer's mouth was tied shut with some rope. Beep had his arm around him.

I watched for a few minutes to get an idea of what the Bone Men were doing. There were eight of them that I could see: one at the door leading to the outside, another at a door leading farther into the fortress, four surrounding Beep and

Saturday - Abandoned Jungle Fortress and the Snow Plains

Killer, one leader sitting down facing Beep, and another one outside that walked back and forth past the windows.

I noticed the leader reading a scroll he held in his hand. While he wasn't paying attention to Beep I saw Beep quietly removing some bones from one of the Bone Men. The archer in charge looked up in time to see what Beep was doing and shouted at him. The Bone Man he had been messing with tried to turn around but had a few too many bones missing. Instead he fell into a heap.

The other Bone Men rushed to his side, and in a flash Hobo the ocelot had landed in the middle of them.

He let out a growl and a scream, and Bone Men were falling in all directions. It seems that Beep had been busy stealing bones!

I jumped down in the middle of the confusion and tore the rope out of Killer's mouth. He immediately began to growl and snarl. I grabbed Beep up and threw him over my shoulder like a sack of potatoes. I looked over to Hobo, and he nodded. He backed up and covered me and Killer, and we scrambled back to the tunnel I had entered from. As we stepped back into the tunnel, Hobo joined us.

We turned around and ran down the tunnel. I could hear arrows being fired at us, that unmistakable whooshing sound they make followed by a ping when they hit the wall. We kept running, then leaped out of the tunnel, into the tree, and climbed down. Arrows were flying all around us by now. Beep was still hanging over my shoulder, thoroughly enjoying his adventure.

Hobo led us through the tangled undergrowth of the jungle to a stream. "Now, listen, Zombie Steve, you take that naughty little boy and don't EVER come back here with him. Do you understand?"

Saturday – Abandoned Jungle Fortress and the Snow Plains

Beep and I laughed. I high-fived Hobo and then dove in the water with Beep and Killer. The three of us swam down the river a little ways, then crossed over. I could still hear the Bone Men coming, and a few of their arrows were flying pretty close to us. That's when I spotted some snow.

"Come on, guys. Head for the snow!" I have a friend, Archie, that's a skeleton archer. He told me once that he can't handle the snow because it makes his bones hurt. I was counting on that.

Beep giggled with glee as we plowed into the snow. I had to pull him out and carry him because the snow was so deep he was getting lost in it. Killer had big feet like snowshoes, so the snow wasn't a problem for him. As we ran deeper into this frozen wasteland, the arrows stopped. I glanced around and saw no sign of the Bone Men.

Well, it was really cold out here. To make things worse, we had just gotten out of the water, and our clothes were getting icy. I don't know much about humans, but I do know that they can get sick if it gets too cold. I quickly built a fire and set Beep and Killer beside it.

I started to build an igloo around us. It would have gone faster if Beep hadn't been so busy eating snow! But soon we had the igloo built. It was daylight just about twenty minutes after I finished. Beep lost interest in eating snow after getting a painful brain freeze, so we ate a meal of potatoes we baked on our igloo/campfire.

"Beep," I said very seriously after our tummies were full, "you sneaked out without me. And Killer, you didn't warn me." Beep and Killer both looked at the ground. "It isn't safe for you to be out there, Beep. Those were bad men that got you."

Beep jumped up, ran over, and threw his arms around my neck. "I know, Zombie Steve. I didn't think it would hurt anything. But then they tied up Killer so he couldn't bite them or protect me, and I knew I was in trouble. But I knew something else, Zombie Steve."

"What was that, Beep?" I asked, carefully untangling him from around my neck. I patted him on his little brown head.

"That you'd rescue me and Killer."

Killer barked, then said, "Oh yeah, and did you ever!"

They proceeded to describe for me, in greatly exaggerated detail, the rescue staged by Hobo and myself. Their version was quite entertaining.

"My Daddy is going to be really impressed with you!" said Beep when he finished.

"You haven't said much about them, Beep. Do you miss them?" I immediately regretted asking that question. Tears started spurting out of Beep's face as he threw himself into my arms. He cried and cried, and I didn't know what to do, so I patted his head, and Killer snuggled up against him and licked his face. Beep finally cried himself to sleep. I could've kicked myself for making him cry.

After Beep fell asleep, Killer explained to me what happened. "It seems that Beep had been naughty again, and his mother told his father. Beep's father was very angry and was going to punish him. Beep thinks they don't love him anymore because he's been so bad, but I rather doubt that. Beep ran off, and that's when he ran into the men that said they were his new teachers and were taking him on a field trip."

Saturday - Abandoned Jungle Fortress and the Snow Plains

"Thanks for telling me, Killer. I agree with you. They are going to be so glad to see him!"

Well, diary, that's all the energy I have to write tonight.

 Diary of a Zombie Steve — Book 1

Sunday
Snow Plains

Zombie Steve here. I woke up to the sound of someone aggressively knocking on the wall of my igloo. I opened the door, making sure not to let Beep out, and came face to face with a mythical creature of legend: Whitey, the infamous snow golem.

"Are you...You aren't..." I stuttered in shock. I had been reading stories about Whitey since I was Beep's size, and my parents always told me he was a myth.

"Yes, yes," he replied in a dignified yet powerful voice. "I am Whitey the snow golem."

"I was always told you were a myth!" I replied.

"You were, it seems, myth-taken." He then laughed at his own joke with a booming laugh so powerful it shook snow off some of the nearby trees. Beep managed to get out with Killer.

"Wow! Whitey the snow golem!" he said, his eyes as big as I had ever seen them.

"Indeed, that has been established. The question is who are you?"

"I am Zombie Steve, Lieutenant of the Zombie Fright Coalition. I am escorting this young man," I said as I pointed to Beep, "back home to his parents. This is our assistant, Killer." Killer wagged his tail, then showed his teeth.

Sunday – Snow Plains

"I have seen the signs requesting the return of the boy. How do I know you are not one of the kidnappers?" asked Whitey, one snow-encrusted eyebrow raised high in a suspicious manner.

"I can vouch for him, sir. He's been helping me to get home and rescued me from the Bone Men," said Beep, standing as tall and straight as he could.

"Indeed, did he now? That explains your presence in my land, Zombie. The skeleton archers find the weather here a bit painful. However, I have come to tell you that you must leave at once. Only snow golems live here."

My jaw dropped, as did Beep's jaw and Killer's jaw. "You aren't the only snow golem?" Beep asked.

Whitey laughed another booming laugh, displacing some more snow from the nearby trees. "Well, where did you think I came from, little man? Of course there are more of us. Few have ever ventured this deep into the Snow Plains"—he paused dramatically and deepened his voice—"and lived to tell about what they saw here." He raised another eyebrow and looked at Beep. This was the first time I had seen Beep even look slightly frightened.

"Wow!" replied Beep. Killer stood up and got closer to Beep, lifting his lip menacingly at Whitey. Brave little wolf that is, I tell you. I wasn't afraid of Whitey, but I respected his legend and authority. If he said we needed to leave, I planned to cooperate.

"Yes, sir, we will be leaving right away." That's when a disturbing thought struck me. How did I know that Whitey wasn't in cahoots with the Bone Men? Could I trust him? Did I dare trust him when I'm responsible for Beep?

Whitey was watching me closely. "I can show you the fastest way out. Follow me."

Diary of a Zombie Steve — Book 1

It didn't seem that we had much choice. I decided I was just being too cautious and turned to go back into the igloo to grab my things. The next thing I knew, something struck me hard on the back of the head, and I fell face first into the snow.

Monday - Bone Yard

Monday
Bone Yard

I woke up in what's known as the Bone Yard. The Bone Yard is the headquarters for—you guessed it—the Bone Men. It's the crumbling remains of an old castle full of stone, vines, and a fair share of booby traps. I found myself in a prison cell with iron bars and an iron door. It was rather dark, but one torch provided enough light for me to decide I was alone down here.

It seems that Whitey the snow golem hadn't been on our side after all. My first concern here wasn't for myself, but for little Beep. Where was he?

I got to my feet and rubbed the back of my head where something had hit me hard enough to knock me out. I noticed the walls between the cells were made of a stone that seemed to be crumbling. Being a cave architect and construction expert, I was able to dig through that wall quietly and quickly. In about ten minutes, I was pleased to discover that I had successfully dug through into a hallway. It seemed fairly well lit, with a torch about every four lengths of block. The hallway itself was about 20 lengths each direction, with a door at each end.

I stood there for a minute to try to decide which way to go. I could go to my left or to my right. I decided to head to the right, but not before I stopped and listened for the telltale sign of rattling bone. I heard nothing. As I started to take a step I spotted a trip wire. One wrong step and I would have been full of arrows!

Carefully I stepped over the trip wire and tried to carefully watch for what might be pressure plates. I reasoned that if they were going to install pressure plates, it would probably be along the center of the hallway, where most people would walk, and not next to the walls. I carefully made my way along the wall to the door at the end of the hall.

As I reached the door, I heard rattling, but just one Bone Man, it seemed. I pressed against the wall so that if someone swung the door open I would be hidden behind it. I held my breath and the door swung inward. As the Bone Man stepped into the hallway I knocked him unconscious, just like they had done to me. I took his bow and arrow for myself and carefully stepped into the hallway he had just come from.

It was very well lit and had doors along each side. I didn't know where to go next when I spotted a block that sure looked like a silverfish stone to me. I kicked it pretty hard, and out popped a silverfish.

"Hey, whaddya think ya doing, ya jerk?" he said in that funny, high-pitched tone that silverfish always seem to have.

"I'm looking for a human boy. Have you seen him?"

"Boy, have I ever! The Bone Men are sure ready for his poppa to pay his ransom, I can tell ya that! Tell ya what, I really shouldn't tell ya where the kid is, but I can tell ya where his pup is. This door right here!" said the silverfish, wiggling over to a solid wooden door. He thumped it twice with his tail, and I heard a muffled bark.

"Thanks, Mr. Silverfish!" I replied, rushing over to the door.

Monday – Bone Yard

"That's MISS SILVERFISH to you, and you're welcome. See ya, wouldn't want to be ya!" were her words, and she disappeared back into a block of stone.

I carefully opened the door and saw Killer Fluffy Butt there, muzzled and looking very distressed. I quickly closed the door behind me (after making sure it wouldn't lock us in) and took the muzzle off Killer.

"Zombie Steve, they've got him! They've got him! I tried my best to fight them off, but there were too many snow golems! You bite 'em and it doesn't do anything but make your teeth hurt from the cold!"

"It's okay, Killer. Whitey took us all by surprise. Can you find him?"

Killer growled and wagged his tail. "You bet, Zombie Steve!" He then started sniffing the air. "By the way, I can smell red stone too. I'll let you know if I smell any more booby traps nearby. And I think most of the Bone Men are on guard duty outside this castle."

I followed Killer down the hall and up a staircase. He stopped me right before a landing. "I smell red stone. I think there's a trap here!"

"Pressure plate," I replied. I hopped over to land on the next set of stairs, and Killer followed me. We reached another landing and found another suspected pressure plate. We hopped over it. It seems the basement dungeon I had been locked in was two floors underground at least.

We finally reached a door at the top of the stairs. We could hear giggling and some angry shouting. Killer and I looked at each other. "Well, I think he's up to his usual," I said. Killer wagged his tail and nodded his head in agreement.

Diary of a Zombie Steve — Book 1

Slowly I opened the door just enough to peek through. I could see the backs of several Bone Men. I would say there were about five in total. One of them had on golden armor, and I figured he was the head of the Bone Men. His name, if memory serves me correctly, was Cranium.

Monday - Bone Yard

Cranium was doing the shouting. It seemed that Beep had been doing his usual, stealing a few bones here and there from the Bone Men when they weren't looking. One of them was lying in a heap on the floor while another tried to figure out where to put the bones back. Killer and I tried really hard not to laugh.

Slowly we watched. Then I noticed, in a hallway off to the side, a glint of light from a trip line. I pointed it out to Killer Fluffy Butt, and he nodded. That could be used as part of our plan. We knew the Bone Men knew about the booby trap, of course, but if they were chasing something they might forget!

I was determined to throw all plans to the side if Cranium laid a hand on Beep, but he just shouted, stomped around, and waved his bony arms. "You have no respect for us, small human. Your father will learn to respect us!" Beep was giggling, watching them try to reassemble the Bone Man he had disassembled. I noticed something clutched tightly in his hand and figured it was one of the bones they needed.

So we had five Bone Men: one was disabled, two were distracted with him, Cranium was shouting his head off, and the last was observing as a guard. We had to get Beep out of there.

I knew I could take Cranium. In fact, Cranium was a bit afraid of me, if I do say so myself. I motioned to Killer, and he lowered himself until his tummy was almost touching the floor. Then he slipped out the door and maneuvered behind Cranium and the guard. Beep saw him, but he's a smart boy and didn't let on. He either kept his eyes on Cranium or the three Bone Men standing next to him. I saw Killer gently toss his head upward.

Diary of a Zombie Steve — Book 1

Beep suddenly threw the bone he had to Killer. In one leap Killer was in the air and had the bone in his mouth. The guard and the two "repairmen" took off after Killer. Killer broke into a run so fast his rear end was touching the ground. I knew

he would head down the hall and under the booby trap. If it took at least one of the Bone Men out, I knew he would be able to get free of them.

As Killer was catching the bone I came bursting through the door in full-on zombie terror mode. I groaned and growled, rushing for Cranium. As I said, he's a bit scared of me. It's something that happened when we were kids, you see. I won't go into it here. He saw me and screamed like a little girl.

Just before Cranium screamed, I heard a snap followed by a whoosh and knew that at least one of the Bone Men had fallen into their own booby trap. I'm sure his scream scared his men half to death. I walked up to Cranium and bodily picked him up. "Beep, disable this skeleton!" I ordered in a scary voice.

Beep followed suit, and instead of giggling began to act like a dangerous little zombie himself. He pulled out Cranium's pelvis, and Cranium's leg and feet bones fell to the floor. I gently laid him down about a foot from his legs. Killer came rushing out and dropped the bone he had in the pile with Cranium's lower extremities.

"They're too scared to come out. This is our chance!" panted Killer. I grabbed Beep and threw him over my shoulder (I knew he wouldn't mind; it always made him laugh like crazy) and we headed down the hall and out the front door that the one Bone Man had been guarding.

We rushed out into the moonlight, and I could tell that morning would be dawning in about an hour. I saw some distant mesas, and so we made a run for them. I doubted the Bone Men would build facilities in a mesa because all the sand tends to get between their bones.

We did get to the mesa, and Killer nabbed us some melons on the way. We ate a delicious dinner, and then I carved us out a shelter and we fell sound asleep. I noticed that Killer was lying across Beep's legs to make sure he didn't get out and get into trouble.

Tuesday
Inside Rainbow Mesa

This morning I decided we should try tunneling through the mesa and out to the other side instead of risking being seen outside. I had sealed up our entrance so well that no one would be able to spot it. I knew this area too. It wasn't too terribly far from Valhalla. Fortunately we had gathered enough melons to keep us fed for quite a while. My only problem was trying to figure out which direction to mine. I knew we needed to go north, but which way was north?

"If we could find some steel, we could make a compass. I got some red stone!" announced Beep.

"Where did you learn to make a compass, little buddy?"

"My dad taught me. He said if I ever get lost, I can make a compass that will point me toward home," he replied. Now, that was a good idea. We were in the side of a hill, so all we needed to do was find some iron.

That's when Killer chimed in. "I can pick up on the smell of iron pretty well. I think if you mine over here," he said, pointing with his nose to a spot along the wall of our shelter, "you'll find some. And some coal too, for smelting it."

 Diary of a Zombie Steve — Book 1

This sounded like a good plan to me. I spent a good portion of the evening mining some iron, making a furnace, and smelting the iron. I decided we could use some weapons and armor to help disguise us. You see, little Beep was starting to look like a little zombie with his ruffled hair and torn clothes. He even had his shirt untucked at just the right angle. Throw some armor on him, and I doubt anyone would suspect he was a little boy instead of a little zombie. This would help us in case we ran into anyone else in the mesa.

By the time everything was smelted and crafted it was almost morning. I watched as Beep expertly made a compass, and I enjoyed the smile on his face when it began to spin. "Home is that way, Zombie Steve!" he said excitedly.

"Indeed it is, Beep. And tomorrow, we are going straight in that direction!"

Until tomorrow!

Wednesday
Deep Inside Rainbow Mesa

Zombie Steve here. We're still deep inside Rainbow Mesa. We haven't encountered any enemies, but we did find what appears to be a forgotten mine shaft...and a forgotten miner!

We (well, I, actually, with little Beep giving orders like he's the straw boss) opened up a mineshaft that was lit with torches. I've found many mineshafts lit with lava, but torches mean someone is in there, and it's not likely to be a mob because we see in the dark.

I was going to cautiously step inside, but Beep dashed in like a bolt of lightning. Fortunately Killer was right behind him. At this point I wasn't worried about someone hurting him; he moved pretty fast. What I was very worried about was having Beep get too close to lava—or water, for that matter. Water in underground caverns can move fast and violently, and lava is not only dangerous to fall into, but it can splash on you.

As I caught up with them I spotted another sign of life: mushrooms!

I was explaining to Beep the dangers of abandoned mines when we heard a cough behind us. There stood an old miner with a diamond pickax slung over his shoulder. "Howdy, fellers. I see that yer both zombers, and I'd really rather that yer didn't hurt me. I'll leave yer alone, and yer leave me alone. Is that er deal?"

 Diary of a Zombie Steve — Book 1

I was pleased he mistook Beep for a zombie, and apparently Beep was too, because he stuck his chest out with pride. "Yes, sir, that is fair enough. We are working our way through the mesa to the north. Is there any way we can help you?"

The miner squinted, placing his pickax on the ground and leaning over on it with both arms. "Now that there is er a good question. Yer don't live in here? Yer didn't spawn in here?"

"No, sir, we did not. We came in and are headed out to the north."

The miner eyed the three of us with suspicion. "Yer didn't, huh? Why did yer come in here in the first place? Were yer running from something…or someone?"

"Yes, sir, we were." I decided to tell him the truth, but not everything. "We have some enemies out there. They threatened the boy," I said, gesturing to Beep. He nodded his head, and Killer tossed his head and barked.

"They sure did, and I'll rip anyone from limb to limb that does it again!"

The miner smiled at Killer. He reached out and petted him on the head. "Yer a good dog, yer are. I had er dog like you once. Named him Terror, er did. We got separated in the cave-in."

Killer smiled. "I wonder…I have an uncle named Terror. He's big and furry with brown spots on his stomach. He said that he once belonged to a very nice miner named Mike."

The miner stood up, surprised. "Meh name is Mike! Would my loyal Terror still be living?"

Wednesday - Deep Inside Rainbow Mesa

Killer wagged his tail vigorously. "Indeed he is! And not a day goes by when he doesn't worry about you! You've got to come with us, Mister Mike."

I wasn't sure how I felt about this development, but it was too late to do anything now. However, with Mike's help we could probably get out of this mesa much more quickly.

"Come on, Mike. I'm Zombie Steve, this is Beep, and this fine dog is Killer."

With that, Mike shared some of his mushrooms with us, and we dug further through the mesa, aiming in the direction indicated by the compass.

 Diary of a Zombie Steve — Book 1

Thursday
Still Deep Inside Rainbow Mesa

Zombie Steve here. We lost so much time today! Here's what happened: We were busy mining a straight line to the north, and without any of us noticing it, Beep had gotten himself a pickax and was mining a side tunnel. We were busy working when we heard a yelp. Of course, Killer took off faster than any of us could. We got to the tunnel, and it was dark. We had been using coal all along to make torches for lighting the tunnels, but I wasn't about to let accident-prone Beep play with fire. So when we got to the opening where Beep was, we couldn't see anything.

"Beep! Killer!" I yelled as Miner Mike headed back to grab some torches. "What's going on?"

"Were tangled up in something, Zombie Steve!" yelled Killer.

"Yeah, and it's sticky and gross!" added Beep.

Mike came in with a torch. He was going to attach it to the wall, but I got into too big a hurry and rushed in without really looking around at all.

I found myself tangled from head to toe in cobwebs. Miner Mike was standing at the door, having lit the room with a strategically placed torch, and was laughing like crazy. "Yer all a sight! I never saw so many critters tangled up in spider webs in my life!"

Thursday - Still Deep Inside Rainbow Mesa

I heard Killer say, "Did you say spider webs? Not cobwebs?"

"Yer right, Killer. These ain't yer ordindary cobwebs. Here's the cave spider coming at yer now!"

Cave spiders are quite a bit different from regular spiders, you see. They are grouchier than regular spiders, and they love to spew this awful, horrible green goo at anything that moves. In seconds we were covered in goo.

"Whoa there, cave spider. This were an accerdent. Now don't you…" Before Mike could finish I saw the spider nail him too.

Then we heard this high-pitched voice as the spider paced back and forth across the room that Beep had discovered. Beep, by the way, was giggling by this point.

"It took me four hours—four hours!—to get those webs woven to custom order, and you idiots come fumbling in here like you own the place and get all tangled up in your smelly clothes and stinky fur!"

I could hear Killer growl.

"Don't you growl at me, you clumsy furball! I am so angry—so angry!—I've got to take a swim to cool off. You had better be out of here by the time I get back!" She stalked out of the room though a doorway, into the darkness.

"Let's get yer outta this mess, fellers." It took Mike about two hours to get us loose. We had just gotten Killer out of the spider webs when we heard that weird spider noise. We ran like crazy back out of the room, closed up the entrance, and collapsed into a tired and sticky heap in our tunnel.

"Well, that were a close one, fellers."

We were so tired all we could do was eat some mushroom soup and go to sleep. I had Killer lie on Beep's legs so Beep couldn't wander off without us knowing about it.

Friday
Inside Rainbow Mesa

Zombie Steve here! Today was what I am certain was the last day we are going to be inside the Rainbow Mesa. I think the lack of sunshine was getting to little Beep, because he seemed depressed and not quite as hyper as usual. Not that Beep wasn't finding ways to get into trouble though. We ran across some silverfish this evening, and he chased them every which way until Miner Mike got so tickled he fell down laughing.

Beep got himself into a very sticky, slimy mess today. We broke into another cavern, and out bounced a bright green slime ball. Beep ran straight for it, and boy, do we have a mess on our hands. We have water to drink but not enough to spare right now to clean him up. And that slime smells just awful—that wretched wintergreen scent!

We worked hard today and haven't encountered any problems. By my estimate we should reach the end of the mesa tomorrow night and Valhalla before dawn.

 Diary of a Zombie Steve — Book 1

Saturday
Outside Rainbow Mesa

Zombie Steve here. It took us a bit longer than I had anticipated to make it out of the mesa, but we made it! I've never been so happy to stand in the nice, cool rays of the moon!

Fortunately for all of us, there was a pond near the mesa. Miner Mike stood guard with Killer while I threw Beep into the water to get cleaned up. I didn't see any sign of the Bone Men, or their leader, Cranium. Things seemed peaceful enough as long as we kept Beep away from the nearby spiders. I then pushed Killer in so he would look white and fluffy again instead of gray and icky. I didn't mess with Miner Mike as far as his personal hygiene went, but I asked him to come with us. We needed as much backup as we could get, because we didn't know what may lie between us and the gates of Valhalla.

Going to the gates of Valhalla took quite a bit of courage on my part. They don't like zombies, you see, and Beep's father especially. However, being an officer in the ZFC did make me an appropriate representative. Our quick jaunt from the mesa to the gates was uneventful. This worried me.

I knocked on the door. "I'm here with Beep, returning him to Major Peter Frightem."

The doors swung open, and a pair of uniformed humans escorted us in. They asked no questions, and that worried me even more.

Saturday - Outside Rainbow Mesa

Ahead of us was a castle-like building, and a man was running out the front doors with a beautiful young woman at his heels. Beep yelled and ran straight for them. My work was done, I thought. Beep is home with his parents.

Smiling from ear to ear, I turned to speak to Killer and Mike when I realized a pair of handcuffs were being slapped on my wrists. Mike was being cuffed also. Killer was being muzzled. Beep's parents had rushed into the castle. I was about to protest my arrest when Cranium walked up.

"Ah, yes! This is the rotten zombie that stole that precious boy Beep from my protection. Here to collect your ransom, eh?" Cranium smirked at me.

I lunged at him, which was a big mistake for a zombie to do in a headquarters full of humans. When I came to, I was in a cell.

 Diary of a Zombie Steve — Book 1

Sunday
Valhalla Prison

Zombie Steve here. I am in a prison cell, and I assume I'm still in Valhalla. I seem to be alone down here. There are about five cells opposite of me and, I assume, four other cells on my side. I called out and there was no answer from the other cells. I have no idea of what time it is. All I know is that when I woke up there was some bread and melons set out for me. Human bread seems a bit bland without gravel to add some spice. The melons were much appreciated, as was the jug of fresh water. I've been awake for what seems like hours, but I haven't seen or heard anyone.

I guess Cranium convinced the humans that I had a part in kidnapping Beep. Beep will set them straight, if they'll listen to him. Grown-ups don't always listen to kids, you know. Surely I'll either be let out soon or put on trial. They don't condemn zombies to life in prison without a trial, do they?

Monday
Valhalla Prison

It's day two in prison for me, Zombie Steve. Again, when I woke up this morning there was food and water. I haven't seen or heard from anyone. I guess I am in solitary confinement, and I hope I'm awaiting trial. Beep will tell them the truth, and so will Killer, and so will Mike the miner. Surely they'll come for me soon!

I have seriously considered trying to mine my way out, but I'm afraid it will make me look guilty. I can't tell night from day, and I am confused, scared, and lonely. Yes, even scary zombies like myself get lonely. If a situation is frightening or disturbing, any normal person or zombie is going to feel fear. What makes someone brave is not giving in to the fear. If I try to escape, I think I might be giving in to the fear. We'll see what happens. At least they let me keep my diary and pencil. I wonder if they read it?

 Diary of a Zombie Steve — Book 1

Tuesday
Home

Zombie Steve here. I noticed that one of the stones in the floor of my cell looked like a silverfish stone, so I struck it. Out popped a wiggly silverfish named Sasso.

"Whaddya want? Whaddya want?" he moaned in their typical high-pitched voice. He seemed to be pretty young, maybe a teenager.

"Can you carry a message for me?" I asked with excitement.

"Maybe. Whatcha give me, zombie boy?"

I didn't really have anything to give him. I thought and thought, but my mind seemed muddled. "I don't know. What do you need? By the way, my name is Zombie Steve."

The silverfish ran back against the wall. "Oh noes, oh noes! The evil kidnapper! Sasso don't need anything from you!" he cried.

"I'm not the kidnapper! I rescued him! Cranium is a liar. Can you at least go to Beep and tell him they have me locked up? I don't think he'd leave me down here like this. Please, you've got to help me!"

Tuesday - Home

Sasso stopped wiggling. "If you're a kidnapper, my parents would not like me carrying a message from the likes of you, would they?" I was right; Sasso was a teenager.

"No, probably not."

Sasso wiggled with excitement and disappeared. I sat there in my cell, staring at my food. I had lost my appetite, and I was so lonely. Suddenly the door at the end of the cell chambers creaked. It was Beep!

"Zombie Steve! Why are you locked up! I didn't know you were here!" Killer was bounding behind him, along with Miner Mike.

Mike broke the lock from my cell, and Sasso popped out. "Hey, ya know what? Ya don't owe me anything." Just as quickly he popped into the floor.

They escorted me upstairs, and this time Beep and Killer were protecting me. I was allowed to present my case before Beep's father, the zombie hunter. I handed him my diary while Beep and Wolf told their side of the story, followed by Mike.

I was released! Right now I am back home in my bed with a medal for bravery pinned to my shirt for returning Beep to his now-grateful mom and dad. Cranium has been put in my cell and is awaiting trial.

Well, this has been some adventure, and it all started with a little human kid named Beep. I can't help but wonder what tomorrow holds!

Diary of a Zombie Steve — Book 1

End

Get YOUR Name Listed on Our Website!

How would you like to be listed in the
Hall of Fame section of our Website?

If that's a YES, then just leave a review for this book on Amazon
with your first name and first initial of your last name.
(Example: Derek P.)

Find Out How Steve Became A Zombie!

www.TheMCSteve.com

Made in the USA
Lexington, KY
26 July 2016